HOW BRIGHT IS YOUR BRAIN?

Amazing Games to Play with Your Mind

MICHAEL A. DISPEZIO

Illustrations by Catherine Leary

Sterling Publishing Co., Inc.
New York

Designed by Dawn DeVries Sokol

Library of Congress Cataloging-in-Publication Data

DiSpezio, Michael A.
How bright is your brain? : amazing games to play with your mind / Michael A. DiSpezio.
    p. cm.
Includes index.
ISBN 1-4027-0651-0
1. Brain–Popular works. 2. Thought and thinking–Popular works. I. Title.
QP376.D577 2004
612.82–dc22

                                                    2004000772

10 9 8 7 6 5 4 3 2 1

Published by Sterling Publishing Co., Inc.
387 Park Avenue South, New York, NY 10016
© 2004 by Michael A. DiSpezio
Distributed in Canada by Sterling Publishing
$^{c}/_{o}$ Canadian Manda Group, One Atlantic Avenue, Suite 105
Toronto, Ontario, Canada M6K 3E7
Distributed in Great Britain and Europe by Chris Lloyd at Orca Book
Services, Stanley House, Fleets Lane, Poole BH15 3AJ, England
Distributed in Australia by Capricorn Link (Australia) Pty. Ltd.
P.O. Box 704, Windsor, NSW 2756, Australia

Sterling ISBN 1-4027-0651-0

Contents

Introduction:
What's in Your Head?

Have you ever thought about thinking? No, this isn't a riddle. It's a real question. Have you ever wondered how a body part that looks like a mushy softball can work as your own personal super-computer control room? Or have you ever wondered how you can bend your fingers or stand on one foot by simply thinking it? Wouldn't it be cool to understand how your brain works?

The human brain (even your little brother's) is very special. For starters, it is incredibly powerful. It can solve equations. It can write symphonies. It can read cool books like this one. In fact, the brain is so awesome that it has the ability to think about thinking. No other living creature's brain can do that. Go ahead, try it. Take a moment to think about that first question. You see what I mean? No dog, no matter how well it can fetch, can do that trick!

The brain is also constantly changing. It responds to new ideas and new thoughts by altering the finer parts of its structure. In fact, you've already rewired some of your brain's tiny connections by reading these first few paragraphs. Would you like to rewire more of your brain? If so, *How Bright Is Your Brain?* is for you! As you'll soon see, this book is a road map to exploring the most amazing part of your body: the brain.

HOW TO SAY iT

Some of the words in this book are hard to say. Rather than test your brain in pronouncing them, we have included a "HOW TO SAY IT" list. The words are spelled out as they sound and the accent is placed on the letters that are uppercase. An asterisk appears by the word the first time you see it in the text.

DISCLAIMER:

We can't promise that reading *How Bright Is Your Brain?* will boost your IQ or get you better test grades. However, when you are finished with this book, you'll know plenty more about your brain and the way it works.

Thoughtful Beginnings

Thoughts. You've been having them for your whole life—even when you're asleep. But what are they? How would you describe a thought? Where do they occur?

We'll start with the easiest question first. Thoughts happen in a very special part of the body: the brain. Although scientists don't fully understand thoughts, they know that thinking involves electrical and chemical signals that travel in the brain. Like electricity moving through a wire, thoughts travel along distinct paths. They don't just float around. But the paths aren't simple. They branch out into a spiderweb–like design. It is this mind-boggling superhighway of connections that forms the unseen structure of the brain.

BRAIN TWISTER

What do a thinking human brain and a glowing low-watt lightbulb have in common?

Answer: They both use about the same amount of power. That's right, your brain uses power just like an ordinary electric lightbulb. In fact, your brain's flow of electrical signals is similar to the movement of charges found in an electric circuit. However, you don't need to be worried about getting electrocuted from your thoughts. Although your brain does produce electricity, the charges are spread out and not very forceful. However, certain devices can detect these electrical patterns and display them as brain waves.

ACTIVITY A Traveling Model

Make a fist with both hands. Bring your fists together so that the heels of your palms are facing each other and touching. Congratulations. You've just built a model of the brain. This one resembles your brain in both shape and size. It's even divided into right and left halves, just like the real thing. Plus, you can take it with you wherever you go.

Following Thoughts

Did you know that scientists can actually "see" the paths of thoughts as they move through the brain? Using high-tech tools, such as PET and MEG scans, scientists can observe and record images of the brain's activity.

Unlike ordinary X rays, these computer-assisted scans can show what parts of the brain are being used. PET, short for positron emission tomography*, uses low doses of radioactive chemicals to highlight areas of brain activity.

MEG, short for magnetoencephalography*, is a newer technique that detects tiny magnetic fields produced by active brain cells. Thoughts traveling along a path of brain cells produce magnetism. Very sensitive instruments detect the magnetic field and display its location on a map of the brain.

positron emission tomography:
PAH-zeh-tron e-MIH-shun toe-MAH-gruh-fee
magnetoencephalography:
mag-NEH-toe-in-seh-fuh-LAH-gruh-fee

HOW TO SAY IT

The Sum of Its Parts

To better understand the brain, scientists divide this body part into different regions. Some of these areas are on the inside of the brain. In other words, you can't see them unless you cut open the brain. Other regions are on the surface. These areas can be identified by their unique pattern of nooks and crannies.

From the outside, three main parts are easy to see. Let's look at each region.

Cerebrum*: In humans, the cerebrum is the largest part of the brain. Although its squished noodle-like appearance isn't impressive, its power is! The cerebrum is where your thoughts happen. Personality, communication, and reasoning arise from the cerebrum. It's also the place that sends out signals that control your body movements.

HOW TO SAY IT

cerebrum:
su-REE-brum
cerebellum:
sair-ah-BELL-um

Cerebellum*: This is the place that helps coordinate your body movements. In Latin, the word translates into "little brain." That's a pretty accurate description of this smaller brain part that is tucked in beneath the cerebrum.

Brain Stem: This region works behind the scenes. It controls automatic actions that you don't have to think about, such as breathing and heartbeat.

CEREBRUM

BRAIN STEM

CEREBELLUM

ACTIVITY Wearable Model

You Will Need

- a bathing cap that you don't need anymore (cheap ones work best)
- nontoxic markers

You can create a wearable brain model. With your nontoxic markers, copy the illustration on this spread to the bathing cap. You'll be the fashion plate of the science class.

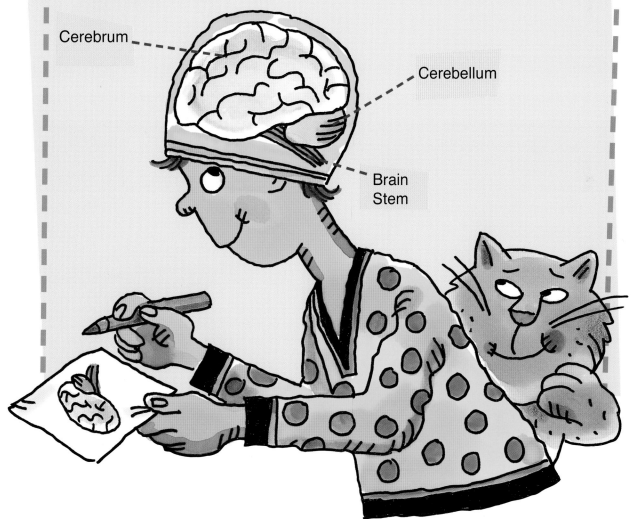

Cerebrum

Cerebellum

Brain Stem

Walnuts and More

Crack open a walnut. What's inside? How about a model of the brain? We're not kidding. The shape and surface of a walnut resembles the features of a brain. Similar to the outside of the nut, the cerebrum is covered with a pattern of grooves and bumps. Although the brain's design looks like a random arrangement, it's not. This surface landscape is mostly the same from person to person.

RIGHT AND LEFT TOO

There's another nutty similarity. Both the walnut and the brain are divided into two side-by-side halves. These halves are called hemispheres*. Although they are similar in appearance, there's a switcheroo that occurs. The brain's right hemisphere controls the left side of your body. Likewise, the left hemisphere controls the body's right side. Each hemisphere also has certain roles that it specializes in. Turn the page to the next spread to see how each works.

HOW TO SAY IT

temporal:
TEMP-ore-ull
occipital:
Ohk-SIP-eh-tull

parietal:
puh-RYE-uh-tull
hemispheres:
HEM-iz-fears

Four-Way Split

Ridges and bumps are used to divide the cerebrum into four distinct regions. These large areas are called lobes. Each lobe has its own specialty.

Frontal Lobe: A good part of your personality lives within the "wiring" of this region. The frontal lobe is also active in problem solving, emotions, and reasoning. In addition, one part of this lobe sends out the messages that control your body movements.

Parietal* Lobe: This part of the brain is active in understanding the sensations detected by the skin. These sensations include heat, cold, pain, and touch. Touch this page and you'll activate this region.

Occipital* Lobe: This part of the brain is dedicated to seeing and understanding the nerve signals sent by the eyes. In fact, it's active right now as you are looking at this page!

Temporal* Lobe: This part is active in hearing and understanding sounds. It also helps produce memories.

Down the Middle

Scientists studying the brain have observed that the right and left hemispheres are in charge of specific functions. The left hemisphere processes the three Rs. That means for most people, it does most of the work when it comes to reading, writing, and arithmetic. It also fairs pretty well with scientific skills.

The right hemisphere has more abstract tasks. It processes thoughts of imagination, insight, music, and art. It's also the emotional half and helps us picture three-dimensional forms.

ACTIVITY Choice Side

Did you know that most people have a preferred hemisphere that they use to think? When they are stressed, they tend to do more of their thinking on this favored side. Which side do you prefer to use? Take the following test to find out.

1. Which type of test do you prefer?

    a. Multiple choice.

    b. Essay.

2. When planning to meet someone, are you usually:

    a. On time or early.

    b. Late.

3. Do you make decisions based upon:

    a. Carefully examining the choices.

    b. Gut feelings.

4. Is your bedroom:

    a. Neat.

    b. Messy.

5. When reading this book, did you:

    a. Read the pages in order.

    b. Jump to the most interesting parts.

Analyzing Your Responses

For each (a) answer, give yourself 1 point. For each (b) answer, give yourself 2 points. If you scored 7 or under, you are a left brain thinker. Most likely, you are very organized in your approach to things. If you scored 8 or above, you are a right brain thinker. Chances are, you think in a less organized way but may have many creative thoughts.

Righties and Lefties

Check out the statements below. One of them is not true. Can you uncover which one is the myth?

a. The Old English word *lyft* meant "useless."

b. During the 1600s, lefties were thought to be witches and burned at the stake.

c. People are mostly right-handed because the brain's left hemisphere is slightly larger.

d. Playing left-handed is forbidden in the sport of polo.

Answers:

a. That's the truth. Historically, the left-handers were never the favored group.

b. True. Like other groups who were different, lefties faced persecution.

c. This is the myth! It sounds like it would make sense since there is a size difference between the hemispheres. The only problem is that the difference is opposite of what's stated above. In most righties, it is the right hemisphere (which doesn't control their favored hand) that is larger.

d. True. Polo prejudice. This ruling is still in effect today. Most likely the anti-lefty law is meant to protect the polo ponies that are trained to expect mallet swings from the horse's right side.

THE TRUTH ABOUT RIGHTIES AND LEFTIES

So a left-handed person's brain doesn't necessarily have a larger right hemisphere and a right-handed person's brain doesn't necessarily have a larger left hemisphere. Then why are some people lefties and others righties? There are many theories, but almost all scientists believe that being a lefty or a righty is something that you are born with.

We humans show a right-handed preference. With typical development, an infant becomes a righty. But if the infant lacks the right-handedness gene (or if it doesn't work correctly), the infant is born a lefty.

ACTIVITY Find the Right Person

Check out the list below. Can you spot the right-handed person?

a. Leonardo da Vinci

b. Marie Curie

c. Julia Roberts

d. Paul McCartney

e. President George W. Bush

f. Oprah Winfrey

Answer on page 77.

Word Power

Do you like to divide things up? Well, so do scientists. The brain regions that you've learned about are only a start. Scientists divide these into even smaller regions. These smaller regions have very distinct roles. One part may identify colors. Another might help us understand words. It makes sense to think that all of these parts get along with each other all of the time. Right? Wrong.

In the 1930s, J. Ridley Stroop discovered that a strange thing happens when the brain receives conflicting information. He named it the "Stroop Effect." Want to see what Dr. Stroop meant?

ACTIVITY The Stroop Effect

Check out the two columns below. Go down each column and identify the color of ink used to print each of these words. Remember, you are not spelling out and reading the word. Instead, you are identifying ink color used to print each word.

Red	Red
Green	Green
Orange	Orange
Blue	Yellow
Purple	Blue
Yellow	Purple
Black	Black
Green	Green

Dribble Mouth

Most likely, you had no problem identifying the ink colors in the first column. It was easy. The color matched the meaning of the word. However, the second column wasn't so easy. Let's look at the first word. A part of your brain called the VPS recognizes the color. It saw green ink and sent a signal that communicated "green." A different region, called the OT, understood the meaning of the word. This part used language to decode the letter and spell out the word "red." When these two messages met, they clashed and produced a "dribble mouth" effect.

Red

VPS

OT

"GREEN"

"RED"

CONFLICT

RED...NO, GREEN...ER, RED...

Building Blocks

Suppose you were able to divide a brain into smaller and smaller pieces. What would you eventually get?

a. In trouble.

b. A big mess (something you couldn't put back together).

c. A look at the brain's building blocks.

Answer: c. Yes, it's the brain's building blocks, but these units are not made of wood or plastic. They are alive! Like other parts of your body, the brain is made up of microscopic parts called cells. Each cell is an independent living unit. Within your body, cells work together. Cells form complex parts that help your whole body stay alive and healthy.

ACTIVITY Modeling Experience

Check out the drawing of a nerve cell on the opposite page. Can you build a model of it?

You Will Need

- a pipe cleaner
- beads
- clay

1. To represent the cell body, shape a lump of clay into a small ball.

2. String a series of beads onto a chenille stick. Twist both ends of the stick to prevent the beads from slipping off the wire. This part will represent the axon.

3. Roll some of the clay into very thin cords. Join pieces of this cord together to form small tree-like "branches." Attach these branches to the cell body. These parts represent the dendrites.

4. Get a student (a friend or family member) and teach that person about nerve cells using the model you created.

Dendrites: Pick up nerve signals from neighboring cells.

Nucleus: The control center of the cell.

Gap: The space between neighboring cells.

Axon: The main path of the nerve cell for carrying the nerve signal.

Cell Body: Has parts that keep the cell alive and healthy.

NERVES

The living building blocks that make up the wiring in your brain are called nerve cells, or neurons*. Neurons aren't only found in the brain. They form a network throughout your body. This network carries the messages between your brain and all your other body parts.

Each nerve cell has a special shape that helps it perform the cell's main function: to transmit nerve signals. One end of the cell has antenna-like branches called dendrites*. The dendrites receive messages from neighboring cells. The opposite end of the cell has a long transmitting cable. This fiber-like part that carries signals away from the cell body is called the axon*.

Of All the Nerve

Your entire body is wired. These cables aren't made of copper wire or optical fiber. The wiring we're talking about is made of nerve cells. Each of these "living wires" is formed by a group of side-by-side nerve cells. To keep these fibers together and help protect them, they are wrapped with a tough covering. The thickest bundle of nerves forms the signal "superhighway" called the spinal cord. The spinal cord extends from the base of your brain to the bottom of your spine. All along its length, the spinal cord connects to nerves that communicate to different body parts.

ACTIVITY You Got to Have Art

Working with a friend, draw a life-size model of your nervous system.

You Will Need

▪ large sheet of paper, wrapping paper, or unwaxed butcher paper
▪ crayons
▪ a friend

1. Cut a sheet of paper that is longer than the height of your friend.

2. Place the paper on a hard, smooth floor.

3. Have your friend lay down in the middle of the paper.

4. Use your crayon to draw an outline of your friend's body.

5. When the outline is complete, use crayons to draw in the nervous system parts that are shown in this diagram. Remember to also copy the labels. You can hang your drawing up in your room or inside your closet door to learn about your nervous system.

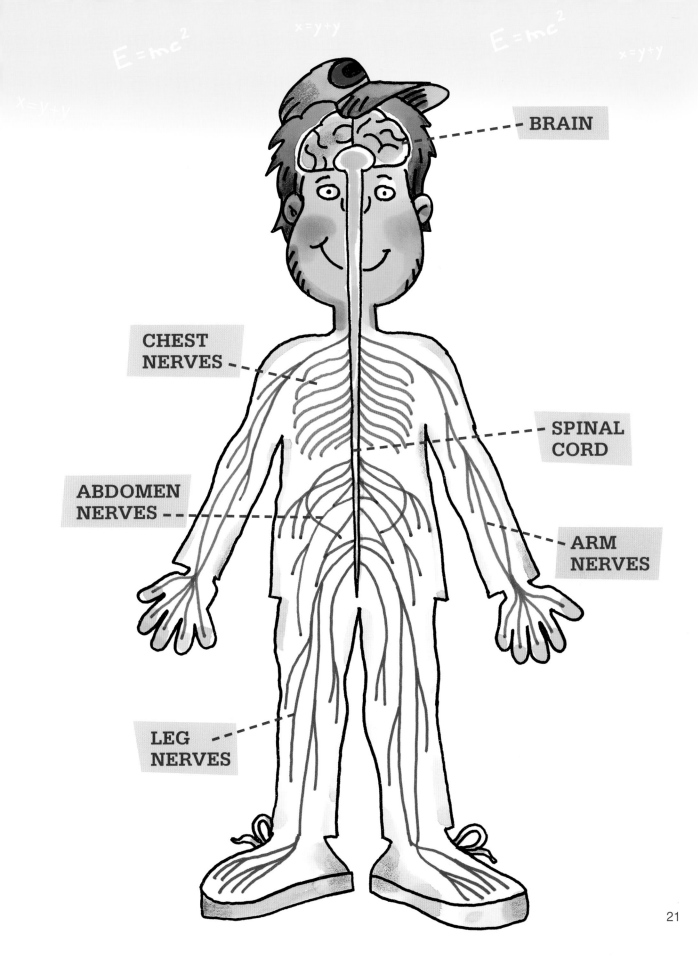

BRAIN

CHEST NERVES

SPINAL CORD

ABDOMEN NERVES

ARM NERVES

LEG NERVES

Two Ways to Travel

Have you ever watched a race called a triathlon? If so, you know that each athlete must run, cycle, and swim as they travel along the race course. Like these athletes, the nerve signal also moves along using different methods of travel. Part of the time, the signal is electrical. Other times, it's chemical.

It's Electric

The signal that travels within a nerve cell is an electrical pulse. It begins when a dendrite is stimulated. The stimulation produces a signal that travels from the tip of the dendrite toward the cell body. Like a jolt of current moving down a wire, this signal sweeps along the cell. It moves across the cell body to the axon. From here, the electrical signal races down the axon toward a neighboring cell.

It's Chemical

At the tip of the axon, the road ends. The space between neighboring cells stops the current dead in its tracks. So now it's time for a change. At the axon tip, the electric signal causes the cell to release chemicals into the gap. These flowing chemicals cross the gap, reaching the dendrites of the neighboring cell. Dendrites that detect this chemical produce an electrical signal in this neighboring cell, and the process continues on.

ACTIVITY Testing Your Signal

This model is a great way for you to see how a nerve signal travels.

You Will Need

- cotton rope, like a clothesline or long jump rope
- small plastic pail
- mailing tape
- plastic packing peanuts

1. Set the pail upright in the middle of the floor.

2. Use tape to attach one end of the rope to the side of the container.

3. Fill the container with plastic peanuts.

4. Hold the other end of the rope and pull it so that it does not droop.

5. Quickly jerk your hand so that you create a pulse in the rope. Watch the pulse advance down the rope.

Analyzing Your Model

1. What happens when the pulse strikes the container?

2. What does the rope represent?

3. What does the pulse represent?

4. What do the plastic peanuts represent?

Answers

4. Chemicals released from the tip of the axon.

3. An electrical signal moving along a nerve cell.

2. A nerve cell.

1. Some plastic peanuts fly out of the pail.

Pain: It's All in Your Head

When you step on a tack, a "pain" signal is created by the injured nerve cells. This signal travels along your nerves to your brain. Like messages that describe temperature or pressure, this signal is a set of electrical impulses. In your head, these impulses are directed to a part of the brain called the ACCx that understands the message as pain.

That's the Rub

Suppose you do step on a tack. One way to relieve the pain is to rub the injury. It really helps. When you rub an injury, you produce a different set of signals that travel to your brain. The rubbing (pressure) signals compete with pain signals for the use of transmission lines to the brain. Since some of the pain signals are replaced by pressure signals, your brain perceives a decrease in pain. So the next time you step on a tack or stub your toe, try this pain-relieving technique.

DATE WITH A DENTIST

The next time you need to see your dentist because you have a cavity, have your parents set up a late afternoon appointment. The amount of pain someone experiences seems to vary with the time of day. At around 6 P.M., most people are less sensitive to the jabs, scraps, and drills that can produce tooth pain. No one knows for certain why this happens. Perhaps it gives the pain pathways a chance to recharge for the next day?

Pins for Pain

Acupuncture* is a technique used to control pain and restore health. Practiced for thousands of years, it is an ancient medical therapy of China and Japan. During an acupuncture treatment, thin needles are inserted just below the skin's surface. The position of each needle targets a specific organ or body part. Once the needle is inserted, it is activated by heat, electricity, chemicals, or by simply turning the needle.

Scientists think that the pain-reducing action of acupuncture can be explained through chemical nerve transmitters. The needles stimulate nerves that release chemicals called endorphins*. Endorphins are natural pain killers. Like morphine and other opiate drugs, they reduce our feeling of pain and discomfort.

POKE AWAY

Although it can produce the sensation of pain in other parts of the body, the brain lacks pain receptors. That's why a surgeon can poke away at the exposed brain of a patient on the operating table. During these "pokes," the patient talks to the surgeon and moves various body parts. This helps the surgeon identify the role of exposed brain regions and increase the accuracy of the surgery.

acupuncture:
ACK-u-punk-chur
endorphins:
n-DOOR-fens

HOW TO SAY IT

Fast and Slow Signals

Have you ever accidentally slammed your thumb with a hammer? Ouch! How about stubbing your toe? Ouch, again! Although the feeling of pain arrives quickly, it isn't instantaneous. There's a fraction of a second following the slam when you don't feel pain. You know, however, that the nasty signal is on its way. A moment later, the pain arrives.

This delay is because of the different speeds at which the touch and pain signals travel. Your nerve signals are not created equal. The quickest signals race along nerves at about the speed of a blazing racecar. Slower signals wouldn't even beat out a fast-moving bicycle. When you stub your toe, the touch sensation moves many times faster than the pain signal. That's why you realize you slammed your finger an instant before the slower nerve message announces the accompanying pain.

ACTIVITY Round About

Gather several friends together in a circle. Hold hands to form a closed loop. Pick one person as the signal starter.

With her left hand, the signal starter squeezes the right hand of the person standing to her left. The person whose hand is squeezed responds by squeezing the right hand of the person to his left. The next person does the same, transmitting the signal down the line. Eventually, the pulse returns back to the signal starter.

You can find out how fast this pulse traveled by making a couple of rough measurements. First, you need to determine the distance traveled. Don't forget that one nerve path carries the feeling of a squeeze from the right hand to the brain. The other nerve path sends the "squeeze command" from the brain to the left hand. Add both paths when calculating the total distance traveled by the nerve message.

The other measurement you'll need is the time for a complete loop of the signal. Once you have the total distance traveled, divide this distance by the travel time. This calculation will give you the speed at which this squeeze was passed along.

Separate Highways

When it comes to transmitting signals, nerves are one-way streets. That's why you have some nerves that carry messages from the body to the brain. The messages that move along these nerves communicate information gathered by your senses. The other type of nerve carries signals from the brain out to the body. These signals control body parts and instruct them when and how to move.

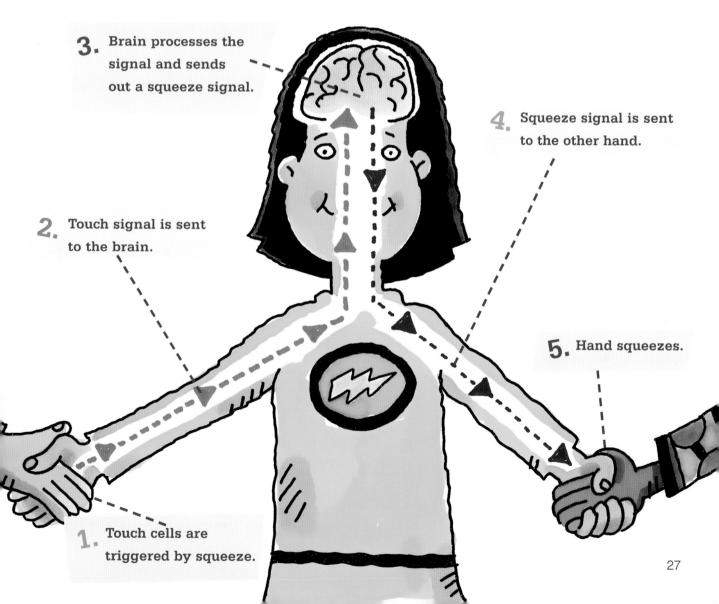

3. Brain processes the signal and sends out a squeeze signal.

4. Squeeze signal is sent to the other hand.

2. Touch signal is sent to the brain.

5. Hand squeezes.

1. Touch cells are triggered by squeeze.

Think Quick

Step up to the plate. The pitcher hurls a fastball moving at 80 mph. You judge the speed and position of the ball. You predict where it will be when it crosses the strike zone. Quickly, you swing the bat. Bam! It's a home run.

That was quick. But although it was fast, your responses weren't instantaneous. It took time for your body to figure out what was happening and how to respond. Part of the delay was caused by the speed at which nerve messages travel and the distance over which they are transmitted.

Your action was also slowed by thinking about how to response. What should you do? Should you swing? Should you respond at all? Maybe it's better to "walk" to first than to chance it by swinging at a ball outside the strike zone? It's a call you have to make—and you don't have too much time to decide.

ACTIVITY Slipping Away

How quickly can you react? Here's your chance to test compare reaction speeds.

You Will Need

- a ruler
- a friend

1. Have a friend pick up a ruler by the end with the highest measurement. While holding this end, let the ruler hang freely.

2. Open up your right hand and spread your fingers.

3. Have your friend position the dangling ruler so that its bottom edge is even with the top of your spread fingers.

4. Without any warning, your friend releases the ruler, letting it slip downward. The moment you see the ruler released, quickly close your hand. Note the "measurement" at which you caught the ruler.

5. Try this three times. Record the ruler's measurement at which your fingers came together each time. To figure out the average, add the three measurement that you got and divide the sum by three. This is the average distance that the ruler dropped before you stopped its fall.

6. Switch roles with your friend and repeat Steps 1 to 5 to find out who's quicker.

Unlike reflexes, which you can't improve because they are hardwired into your system, you can improve your response when trying to catch something. Practice makes perfect. Even visualizing the task results in better performance.

BRIGHTNESS MATTERS

Your eyes have special cells that sense light energy. When these cells are triggered by light, they send off a signal to the brain. The quickness at which the cells send the message depends upon brightness. A well-lit object triggers these cells quickly. A dimmer object takes longer to trigger the cells.

Suppose you wanted to explore the connection between brightness and reaction speed. How would you change the ruler activity into an experiment that might be used in a science fair?

Brainless Circuits

So far, you've learned about signals that travel from the body to the brain and from the brain to the body. But did you know that some nerve paths don't include the brain? That's right. Brainless circuits.

Have you ever seen a doctor strike a patient's knee with a rubber hammer? In response, the knee jerked upward! This "knee-jerk" response is called a reflex, or reflex action. It occurs when a message "short circuits" and doesn't go to the brain. In the case of reflexes, short circuits aren't bad. In fact, they help you respond quicker by not having to think about what you are doing.

Pick a Path

When a knee gets struck by a rubber hammer, a signal of the impact is produced. This signal travels along nerves from the knee to the spinal cord. When it reaches the spinal cord, the message splits and follows two paths.

The longer path goes up the spinal cord to the brain. There, the brain processes the signal. It "feels" the pressure of the blow and you become aware of the hammer's impact. It might even make you say, "Ouch."

The shorter path doesn't travel up the spinal cord. Instead, it enters the cord and transfers its message to a "movement" nerve. This nerve goes out of the spinal cord to the leg muscle. It is the impulse from this short circuit that causes the knee to jerk.

Since this second path was much shorter, its action is much quicker. In fact, the knee jerks *before* your brain is aware of it.

ACTIVITY Auto Pupil Control

You Will Need
- a friend
- a room with various lights

Since getting struck with a rubber hammer might be uncomfortable or cause injury, we'll take a look at another reflex action. This one occurs in your eye.

Your eye has an opening that allows light to enter. This opening is called the pupil. Surrounding the pupil is a muscle called the iris. The iris contains colored pigments. The pigments in the iris make a person's eyes appear brown, blue, or green.

Like all muscles, the iris can contract and expand. When the iris contracts, it gets smaller and shrinks away from the center of the eye. This causes the pupil to get bigger. When the iris expands, it enlarges toward the center of the eye. This causes the pupil to get smaller. The contraction and expansion of the iris is automatic. You don't have to think about it. Like the knee-jerk reaction, the change in pupil size is a reflex action.

You can see this research by observing the eye of a friend in a dimly lit room. Note the size of the pupil in dim light. Then have someone turn on the room's bright lights. What happens to the size of the pupil?

CAUTION: Do not shine a bright light or laser into the eye! This can cause permanent damage.

All in the Wiring

Connections, connections, and more connections. It's all in the wiring. Your brain contains about 100 billion nerve cells. Although 100 billion sounds like a huge number, it's incredibly small when you compare it to the number of connections made by these cells.

Consider this: some brain cells can create up to 10,000 connections to neighboring cells! So signals have 10,000 possible paths into a single cell. Once the nerve is stimulated, it passes this message to its neighbor. Again, each neighbor offers a choice of 10,000 new routes to follow. On and on the message is transmitted until it finally stops.

It's this awesome number of possible thought paths that gives a brain its thinking power. Some scientists estimate that the number of paths is equal to the number of atoms found in the entire universe.

EQUAL TIME FOR OTHER CELLS

In addition to nerve cells, there are other cells in the brain. In fact, the most numerous cells in the brain aren't nerve cells at all. They are called glial* cells. Scientists estimate that there are between ten to fifty times more glial cells than nerve cells!

Glial cells don't carry nerve messages. They do, however, support the nerve cells and make sure they stay healthy. Some glial cells help bring food to nerve cells. Others get rid of waste and dead cells.

HOW **TO SAY IT**

glial:
GLEE-al

ACTIVITY Puzzling Connections

Want to see how connections add up?

Check out the pattern of cells shown here. Start up at the top and trace out a path that goes with your finger down the entire pattern. You can't go back up, only down. How many possible paths can you trace from the top cell down to the bottom row?

Answer on page 77.

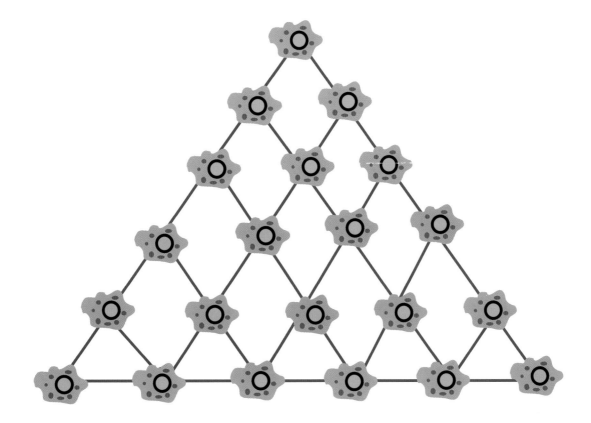

Protecting the Goods

Whether you want to or not, you're wearing a crash helmet. It's called a cranium*. The cranium is a brain "vault" that is formed by the eight curved bones of your skull. Together the bones produce a rigid shell that protects your soft, squishy brain from injury.

But your brain is too important to be protected only by bones. There are other defense systems at work. Lightly tap the top of your head. What do you feel? Hair. Not only a stylish covering, hair acts like a shock absorber to soften bangs and bashes to the cranium. Hair also insulates your head to protect it from temperature extremes.

In addition to your scalp, there are several layers of tissue that cover the brain on the inside. Plus, the brain floats in a special fluid. This fluid protects the brain from sudden shocks and prevents it from bumping into the bones of the cranium.

KEEP OUT!

The blood vessels in your brain are also special. They have densely packed walls with few spaces in between. This packing forms a barrier that prevents most germs and chemicals from leaving the blood. Only a few special molecules, such as oxygen and carbon dioxide, can pass through this blood brain barrier.

Holes in Your Head

Brain surgery was first performed by:

a. Two surgeons in London.

b. The Three Stooges in Hollywood.

c. Prehistoric Peruvians.

Answer: c. Prehistoric Peruvians. Four thousand years ago, the Inca Indians of Peru learned the basics of brain surgery. In a technique called trepanning*, they cut a hole into the skull. This hole helped reduce pressure that was building up on the brain. It was also a way to remove any blood clot that had formed below a bashed-in skull. (Remember, these guys didn't hesitate to club each other in battle.)

We know trepanning was successful because scientists have found prehistoric skulls with holes that had healed. Apparently, the patients survived long enough for healing to take place. In fact, some skulls had several healed holes. Some people never learn.

HOW TO SAY IT

cranium:
KRAY-nee-um

trepanning:
tri-PAN-ning

ACTIVITY Hairy Cushion

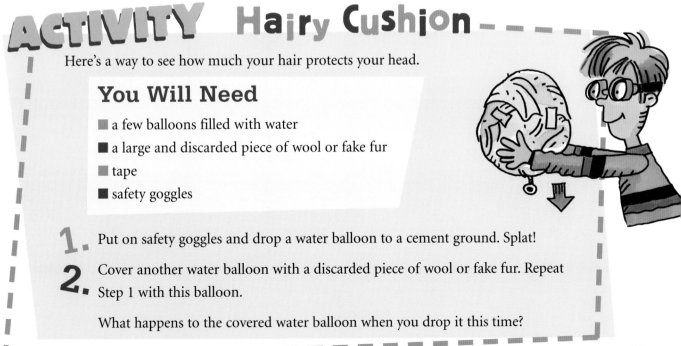

Here's a way to see how much your hair protects your head.

You Will Need

- a few balloons filled with water
- a large and discarded piece of wool or fake fur
- tape
- safety goggles

1. Put on safety goggles and drop a water balloon to a cement ground. Splat!

2. Cover another water balloon with a discarded piece of wool or fake fur. Repeat Step 1 with this balloon.

What happens to the covered water balloon when you drop it this time?

Animal Brains

Which animal has the largest brain?

a. Killer whale

b. Elephant

c. Dolphin

d. Human

Answer: b. An elephant has the largest brain. It weighs about five times more than a human brain. You may wonder then, how come elephants aren't writing these books?

Good question. Larger brains don't necessarily mean more intelligence. Larger animals need bigger brains to maintain their bodies. Some of the extra brain is used to understand the signals sent by sensory nerves. Another part of the brain is needed to control the much larger body of the animal.

BRAIN QUALITY

Some scientists think there is another part to animal intelligence. It's brain quality. How good is an animal's brain? Do all brains function the same way? Some animals might have brains with better connections or faster signals.

$-5Y \times 7Y = -35Y^2$

A Better Way

It seems that there is a better way to compare the brains of different animals. Scientists take into account the size of the entire animal. So if an elephant has a huge brain, you need to consider the animal's massive size.

When the brain weight is compared to the animal's total body weight, things change. Using this method, here's how different brains stack up according to weight and animal size.

1. Human
2. Dolphin
3. Elephant
4. Killer whale

The list puts things in perspective. Plus, it places us at the top of the list. But is this way of dealing with intelligence fair to other animals? From our perspective it is. If other animals were smart enough to make their own list, they would probably place themselves at the top!

3 LBS.

HUMAN BRAIN STATS

The adult human brain weighs about 3 pounds (1.4 kilograms). If you take into consideration the person's entire body weight, we come up with a brain-to-body ratio of about 2%. With this system, the next nearest "brainy" animal is the dolphin. Dolphins score a little less than 1% on this scale. Elephants score a lowly 0.15%.

IQ

Most likely you have heard of IQ. It's short for Intelligence Quotient. A person's IQ is a number that shows how well they performed on a few mental tests. Although there are many types of mental abilities, IQ tests explore only a limited number of abilities. Most people have an IQ that falls in the range between 95–105. Those with IQ scores above 140 are considered geniuses. But remember, there are all kinds of genius, much of which can't be measured.

Intelligent History

Did you know that widespread testing for intelligence first became common during World War I? At that time, the United States was faced with evaluating the best military position for millions of men that were drafted. Should a draftee be assigned to the infantry? Should he be trained as a pilot? Should he be sent to officer school? To help decide, the army created and gave out an intelligence test. Unlike today's IQ scores, these results weren't given a number value. Instead, the scores were distinguished by a letter grade from A to E.

After the war, interest and use of IQ tests increased. The tests were given in schools and during job interviews. At the time, people believed that a person's intelligence could accurately and completely be described by a number.

In the 1960s, people began to doubt how valid these tests were. These days, the test scores are accepted as more of a measure of how someone performs on a test than as a tool to measure thinking and reasoning. Although a variety of IQ tests are still given, most people understand the limits of standardized testing. Chances are you've taken some sort of standardized verbal or math test. If not, hang in there, because you just may. A form of IQ test still faces most American students applying for college. It's called the SAT (Scholastic Aptitude Test). Although it has evolved over the years, the SAT remains a standardized and impersonal test that assigns a number value to performance.

ACTIVITY IQ Test

What kind of questions are on an IQ test? Are they mostly math problems? Do they include logical thinking? How about word definitions? The definitive answer is "it depends."

There are all sorts of IQ tests. The classic IQ tests have a foundation in math skills and verbal understanding. Often, the basics include logical reasoning and general knowledge. Other IQ tests explore things such as predicting how an object might look when it is rotated in space or uncovering how you use logic.

Here is an assortment of questions similar to those presented on IQ tests. Some are easy. Others are more difficult. You won't be able to figure out your IQ from only a few questions, but this will give you a good idea about what an IQ test is like.

1. Which one of the five makes the best comparison? Dog is to puppy as cat is to:

LION   FELINE   CUB   BABY   KITTEN

2. Which of the five is least like the other four?

STARFISH   JELLYFISH   SHARK

SQUID   ANT

3. Which of the following is least like the other four?

a. ☐   b. ⬠   c. △   d. ○   e. ◇

4. What is the next number in the following series?

$$1 - 1 - 2 - 3 - 5 - 8 - ?$$

9   10   11   12   13   14

5. Which of these six letters is least like the other five?

A   C   E   F   G   H

6. If you rearrange the letters "CARFIA" you would get the name of a:

BIRD CITY COUNTRY PET CONTINENT

7. If two birds can eat two worms in two hours, how many hours will it take three birds to eat three worms?

ONE-HALF   ONE   TWO   THREE   FOUR

8. Which of the five is least like the others?

CANADA   UNITED STATES

SWITZERLAND   MEXICO   NORWAY

9. Which one of the five makes the best comparison?

Jelly is to jam as jam is to:

GRAPE   PEANUT BUTTER
PRESERVES   GELATIN   JELLY

10. Which of the five designs is least like the other four?

Answers on page 77.

Multiple Intelligences

Nowadays, our view of intelligence isn't limited to reasoning and problem-solving skills. It is most often thought of as several different types of thinking abilities. These different thinking styles are called multiple intelligences.

EQ, BRUTE

Have you ever heard of an EQ test? EQ stands for emotional quotient. Like IQ, it's another number that attempts to predict how you'll succeed in life. But instead of measuring traditional math and verbal skills, it measures your emotional responses. Also unlike an IQ test, there aren't any "right" or "wrong" answers. Here's a type of question you might find on an EQ test.

Your teacher lost your only copy of an assignment you handed in. Your response is:

a. You get angry and refuse to do any more work.

b. You rewrite the assignment without asking.

c. You speak with the teacher and ask how you should proceed.

d. You accept the average class grade.

ACTIVITY An Intelligent Assortment

We've listed eight different intelligences below. We've also listed the skills and characteristics of these thinking abilities. Check out these lists, then match each of the intelligences with its characteristics.

1. Language

2. Logic and Numbers

3. Visual

4. Movement

5. Musical

6. Understanding Others

7. Understanding Yourself

8. Naturalist

Answers on page 77.

a. The ability to think in pictures. Enjoys looking at maps, photos, videos, and movies.

b. The ability to understand one's own weaknesses and strengths. Enjoys analyzing one's own dreams, actions, and relationships.

c. The ability to think in words. Enjoys talking, listening, and writing.

d. The ability to think and use numbers, patterns, and logic. Enjoys experiments, problem solving, and doing math.

e. The ability to sense the feelings of others. Enjoys cooperating with others, understanding how others feel, noticing people's moods, observing behaviors, and stopping fights.

f. The ability to classify the things around them. Enjoys observing animals, collecting plants, studying rocks, and comparing and contrasting objects in their surroundings.

g. The ability to control body movements with fine coordination. Enjoys dancing, sports, acting, and crafts.

h. The ability to use sounds in producing and understanding music. Enjoys singing, playing instruments, and writing music.

Brain Games

So now you know that IQ tests aren't the only brain exams out there. In addition to these classic tests, there are exams that explore other parts of your thinking. Some of these tests look at your approach to problem solving: *Do you jump to conclusions? Do you make conclusions based on what you observe? Do you rule out unlikely solutions?*

Other tests try to assess your personality: *Do your emotions help or hurt your decisions? Do you use intuition? Do you make fair judgements?*

There is even a special set of tests that people take to find out what profession they are best suited for. These tests include questions that explore a person's interests. They also look for strengths and weaknesses in both IQ and EQ concepts. Using this information, the tests try to predict how successful and happy a person will be in a variety of professions.

Check out the questions on this spread. Unlike classic test items, these questions engage puzzle-solving skills. To answer them, you need to critically examine each situation and arrive at a unique solution. Is your thinking powerful enough to take on these puzzling challenges? There's only one way to find out.

ACTIVITY
Riddle Me This

This puzzle poem comes from a Mother Goose collection that was printed in the 1700s. Can you figure out the answer?

As I was going to St. Ives,

I met a man with seven wives,

Every wife had seven sacks,

Every sack had seven cats,

Every cat had seven kits;

Kits, cats, sacks, and wives,

How many were going to St. Ives?

Answer on page 77.

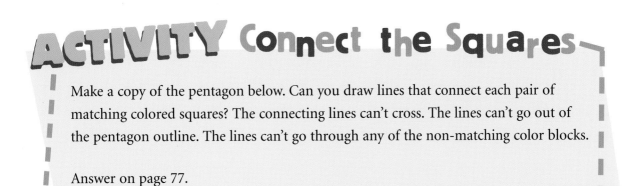

ACTIVITY Connect the Squares

Make a copy of the pentagon below. Can you draw lines that connect each pair of matching colored squares? The connecting lines can't cross. The lines can't go out of the pentagon outline. The lines can't go through any of the non-matching color blocks.

Answer on page 77.

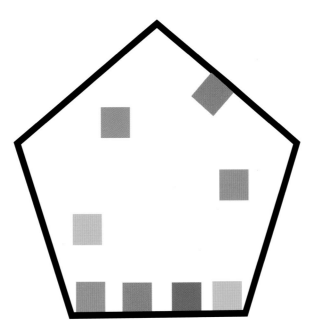

Creativity Rules and Breaks Rules

Everyone has the ability to be creative. However, for most of your early years, this inventive way of thinking isn't nourished. Instead, you are told to follow along, get in line, and do what has been done before. Your thoughts "come together" based on what is logical and common. This type of thinking is called convergent* thinking. Although it can be pretty powerful in the way it organizes and analyzes thoughts, it doesn't create new ideas.

STIMULATING CREATIVITY

Looking for creative ideas? Then take a walk. Physical exercise can often stimulate creativity. Some people take hot baths, others relax and listen to music. Still others just sit outdoors and daydream. Ludwig van Beethoven, an 18th-century composer, had a different approach to creativity. Before he sat down to write music, he dumped ice water on his head!

The type of thinking that comes up with brand new ideas is called divergent* thinking. When you use divergent thinking, you move away from the expected. Your thoughts go out in new directions and make unexpected connections. These connections are the foundations of creativity.

Creativity often starts with seeing something that everyone else sees. However, you see it differently. But that's only the start, because creativity is not passive. It may begin with observing, but it also requires some doing or motivation. You have to have drive to be creative, otherwise, you passively accept what is at hand. It takes a lot less brain power to watch TV than to create a work of art.

The next question then is: where does this motivation come from? Are creative people told to be creative? Hardly. Most

HOW TO SAY IT

convergent:
con-VER-jent
divergent:
die-VER-jent

artists and creative geniuses say that it comes from "within." They have an inner drive to express this difference. Often, there is a strong emotional connection that can be seen in the final product of their work.

Here's a sample of creativity that uses familiar words. Notice how the meaning of each word is expressed in the way its letters are drawn and arranged.

ACTIVITY Word Play

Now it's your turn. Draw the following words in some way that expresses their meaning.

You Will Need

- pencil
- paper

Fire

Smile

Cup

Bookworm

Mountain

Dot

Chair

Finding Creativity

Where is creativity located? Is there a special part of the brain that generates "creative thoughts"? Although no one knows for certain, creativity seems to be a "side thing." As you've learned, the brain is divided into two sides, or hemispheres. The right half of the brain is the "emotional" and "free-spirited" side. Within this hemisphere, the brain generates fresh, new ideas. However, once the ideas are generated, they need to be tested. The testing is done by the left half of the brain. In this more logical and analytic half, the ideas are examined and verified.

Creativity also depends upon several parts of the brain that work together. These brain parts belong to something called the limbic* system. The limbic system is where emotions are formed. It is also responsible for the "drive" you have to pursue creative goals.

HOW TO SAY IT

limbic:
LIM-bik

ACTIVITY Riding a Horse

Here's a great puzzle that gets you thinking out of the box. It's based upon the "Trick Donkeys" puzzle that was created by Sam Lloyd over a century ago. Lloyd's puzzle was so popular that it made him a millionaire!

You Will Need

■ a photocopy machine
■ scissors

1. Make a copy of the three pieces of the puzzle.

2. Use scissors to cut out and separate the three separate sections.

3. Arrange the three sections so that the cowgirl and cowboy sit on top of a horse. You can't cut or bend these pieces. You can only arrange them so that two complete horses and their riders are shown.

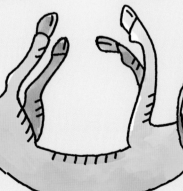

Answer on page 78.

Staying Out of the Box

Think of a creative person, some real genius. How would you describe that person? Are there things that this person might have in common with other highly creative people? Is so, what are those traits?

Psychologists have tried to uncover similarities among creative geniuses. So far, they found the following things that many geniuses seem to share:

- They have a child-like view of life.
- They can be completely absorbed in their creative work.
- Their creativity occurs in bursts.

ACTIVITY   Loop Trick

You Will Need

- a strip of paper
- scissors
- small piece of tape

Check out the picture of this loop. Pay special attention to the paper "shelf" that bends out from the loop. The loop is made from a single strip of ordinary paper. Its ring shape is secured by a small piece of tape at the far end.

Answer on page 78.

Now that you know what it looks like, it's your job to build a copy of this shape.

Do you have any of these traits? If so, perhaps you're already a genius, or you're maybe on your way to becoming one now. Many people with very high IQs show their genius at an early age. Wolfgang Mozart, an 18th century composer, started writing music at the age of 5. Albert Einstein studied college level math when he was 12.

In the meantime, here are several puzzles that may help you stretch the way you think.

ACTIVITY No Lifting Allowed

You Will Need

- Photocopy machine or markers
- pencil

Photocopy or redraw this puzzle on a piece of paper. Place your pencil on the red dot that is in the middle of the top line of this nine-dot pattern. Without lifting your pencil from the paper, can you connect all nine dots with only four straight lines? Remember, you can't lift your pencil from the paper—where one straight line ends, the next must begin.

Answer on page 78.

Thanks for the Memories

Can you remember a telephone number? Most likely, memorizing a series of seven digits isn't too difficult. But how about memorizing a sequence composed of over 30,000 digits?

In mathematics, there is a symbol, π. It represents a number that relates the measurements of different parts of a circle. The number is usually rounded off as 3.14. However, its exact value has a limitless number of digits. For those of you who want a challenge, you can try memorizing the first twenty digits of pi:

3.1415926535897932384

Obviously, there are tricks to memorizing 30,000 digits. One trick replaces numbers with memorized words. The sounds in each word represent a number. The next step is to create a huge poem that uses these words. As you probably know, a structured poem is easier to remember than a series of random numbers. When the poem is recalled and recited, the words are decoded back into numbers.

Another memory trick links numbers to the images in a memorized story. Like the previous trick, this one is based upon words to store related numbers. However, in this case, visual images (and not lines of poetry) are remembered.

3.141592653589793238 4

WHEN TIME MATTERS

The greatest number of random digits memorized in only 4 seconds is over twenty!

Chunking

Another memory trick uses chunking. Phone numbers are "chunked" together into three-digit and four-digit parts. This makes memorizing complete seven-digit number easier to do. Listen for this chunking when someone recites a phone number. Can you think of other sequences that are divided into chunks?

ACTIVITY   Memory Walk

Another trick that can boost your memory is called a "memory" walk. Here's how it works.

Suppose you had to memorize the following list of ten random words: Parade, Car, Finger, Red, Washroom, Poster, Computer, Sweater, Elephant, Stream. The hard way is to keep repeating or writing the list. With all the repetition, you might memorize the ten unrelated words.

An easier (and more enjoyable) method is to create a story that connects the words. It might go something like this: *Imagine you went to a parade. You drove there in a car. When you left the car, you slammed the door and caught your finger. It turned red. You ran to the washroom to treat it. On the way, you passed a poster. The poster had a picture of a computer. A display on the computer had an image of a clown wearing a turtleneck sweater. The clown was sitting on top of an elephant. The elephant was drinking from a stream.*

Using this method, now try and create a story to memorize these ten words: Radio, Ocean, Dog, Chair, Flower, Blue, Hand, Mother, Pizza, Robot.

Sleep Tight

By the time a person reaches 75 years of age, they've slept away 25 years! That's right, one-third of your life is spent sleeping. And what do you have to show for it? How about your health?

Although no one knows for certain, it seems that sleep is necessary to restore the body. After a day of activity, your body needs to recover from all the work it put in. Cells need to be repaired. Muscles need to rest. Your brain needs quiet time. Sleep gives you this opportunity to go on "cruise control."

Remembering Dreams

Everyone dreams. Scientists think that dreaming may be the way your brain puts together stray daily thoughts. Others believe that it is the time when you can think about all sorts of things without feeling guilty.

Since dreams seem to fade away quickly, you might want to keep a record of your thoughts in a dream journal. You can create a journal using a pad and pencil, computer, or tape recorder. It doesn't matter what you use, as long as you keep it by your bedside. As soon as you wake up, record your thoughts. Don't forget to include color information, since color may be the first part of the dream to fade away.

ACTIVITY Built-In Alarm Clock

Some people say they have a built-in alarm clock. They can go to sleep and wake themselves up at a certain time. Can you? Pick a day when you do not have to go to school or anywhere else. Tell your parents that you are doing an experiment. The night before, go to sleep when you feel tired. Wake up the next morning without an alarm clock. Are you a natural early bird or night owl?

Early Birds and Night Owls

Did you know that your brain is on a cycle? Don't look for handlebars or foot pedals. The cycle that your brain is on is an activity cycle. Your activity cycle is in sync with daytime and nighttime. During the day, you are up and awake. At night, you rest and sleep. Even without seeing the sun or sky, your brain sticks to the cycle of telling you when to sleep and wake.

People who are early birds have an activity cycle that begins early in the day. Their brain's "wake-up" alarm tells them to be active early in the morning. People who are night owls have a later start to their activity cycle. They wake later in the day and stay up later at night.

Jetlag

When it's noontime in New York, it's 6 P.M. in Paris. That's because these cities are in different time zones. When you fly across time zones, your brain doesn't immediately reset its activity clock. Instead, it resists the time change and tries to maintain its old activity cycle. This can cause a condition called jetlag. People with jetlag can be ready for bed at noontime and feel wide awake at midnight. Although it is bothersome, you get over it. Within a week, your brain readjusts to local time and resets your body's activity clock.

REM

Although a person may be sleeping, they may not be dreaming. Dreams are limited to a stage of sleep called REM. REM is short for Rapid Eye Movement. During this period, your closed eyes dart back-and-forth. At the same time, your brain can experience dreaming. Most people enter the REM stage three to four times during the night. Scientists think that everyone dreams in color. People who say that their dreams are black and white may just be forgetting the colors.

ONE UP, ONE DOWN

Like your brain, the dolphin's brain is split into two hemispheres. When you sleep, both hemispheres go into this state. In dolphins, it appears that only one hemisphere sleeps at a time.

The Real World

Your brain is plastic. That doesn't mean that it is made of the same material as a *Star Wars* model. It means that your brain can change the way it organizes your thinking. By updating thought pathways, your brain creates a mindset that best reflects your latest experiences.

ACTIVITY Reality Flip

Let's explore how your mind's-eye view is tweaked to fit your real-world experience. We can do this by constructing a pinhole viewer that copies the way light rays are cast within the eye.

You Will Need
- large paper cup
- scissors
- pushpin
- rubber band
- wax paper

1. Use your pushpin to punch a pinhole in the center of the cup's bottom.
CAUTION: Be careful using the pin. Its point is sharp.

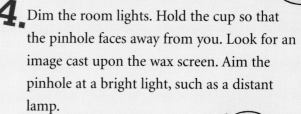

2. Cut out a piece of wax paper that is slightly larger than the cup's mouth. The extra paper should extend about 1 inch (2.5 cm) beyond the rim of the cup in all directions.

3. Position the wax paper so that it is stretched tight across the mouth of the cup. Place your rubber band over the paper and secure it just below the cup's rim. This should keep the wax paper in place.

4. Dim the room lights. Hold the cup so that the pinhole faces away from you. Look for an image cast upon the wax screen. Aim the pinhole at a bright light, such as a distant lamp.
CAUTION: Never look directly at the sun! It can cause permanent damage to the eye.

5. Examine the image that is cast upon the wax screen. What do you see? Do you notice anything topsy-turvy about its appearance?

Of Pinholes and Eyeballs

Like the pinhole viewer, your eye gets an upside-down view of the world. This image is cast upon the retina*—the eye's light-sensitive screen. But even though the retina detects a flipped over world, your brain interprets what you see as right-side up. Without being aware of it, your brain flips the upside-down image around to fit the logical arrangement of the world.

Flipping Experiment

Years ago, scientists created special goggles that flipped views upside down. They gave these goggles to volunteers who wore them whenever they were awake. At first, these subjects where confused and dizzy because they saw a completely upside-down world.

But then it happened! After several days, the world flipped around. Even though they were wearing the upside-down glasses, the brain changed the mind's view into a right-side up world.

Then the subjects removed the glasses. Guess what? Their brains had become used to the new view. Now (without the special goggles) they saw an upside-down world. However, after a few days, the brain once more adjusted and produced a right-side-up image.

retina:
REHT-in-ah

HOW TO SAY IT

Optical Overload

Your brain is overloaded with all sorts of information from what you see. To best deal with the excess information, it uses all sorts of shortcuts. Most of the time, the processing shortcuts work. They get rid of the unnecessary information and concentrate on only the important things. Other times, however, the shortcuts don't work. They produce something that isn't a mind's-eye copy of the real world. These wrong interpretations of reality are called optical illusions.

ACTIVITY Imaginary Sights

Carefully examine the image shown here. How would you describe the central square? Are the edges that form its outline straight or wavy? Is the square slightly lighter or darker than its background?

Most likely, you described a straight-edged square that is slightly brighter than its background.

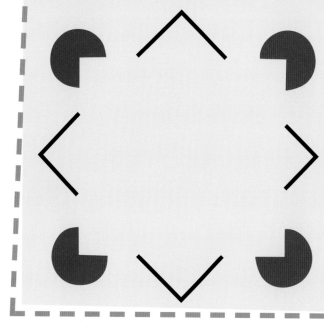

Too bad it doesn't exist! There is no square illustrated in this image. The only place the square exists is in your mind.

Your brain was tricked into creating an imaginary square. It looked at a confusing pattern of shapes and tried to make sense out of it. The most likely explanation was that a square was covering up the arrangement of lines and circles. That "suggestion" was all that was needed. Your brain finished the job by creating an imaginary square.

ACTIVITY Face-Flipping Photo

Without spinning the page around, how would you describe the expression on my face? Am I happy? Sad? Confused? Take your time. Then spin the book around so that my head is right-side up. Pretty strange, eh?

Once more, we have information overload. Your brain is so overworked when looking at my upside-down head that it doesn't realize that the eyes and mouth are inverted. When the head is right-side up, however, it can correctly process the image and uncover the weirdness.

57

Flicker Fusion

Did you know that the smooth action you see in movies, TV, and videos is an illusion? That's right. These fluid movements are imaginary—the product of a confused brain.

Suppose you were looking at a picture that was suddenly replaced by a different picture. What would you see? Most of us would observe two different and separate pictures, one replacing the other. Replace this second picture by another and we'd see a third distinct image in a sequence of changing pictures.

At a moderate rate, your brain can tell the individual images apart. It processes each picture as a separate and distinct form. However, if the images are changed at a fast enough rate, the brain can't keep up. It no longer "sees" separate images. Suddenly, the sequence of pictures fuses into the illusion of smooth motion.

ACTIVITY Frame-Flipping Fun

Let's create an illusion of smooth motion.

You Will Need

- a photocopy machine
- scissors
- a clip binder

1. Make four photocopies of this series of frames on the opposite page.

2. Use scissors to carefully cut out each frame.

3. Assemble each stack of eight frames. Keep them in order so that the sequence begins with "1" on the top and proceeds through "8" on the bottom-most frame.

4. Stack the sets of eight frames on top of each other so that the "1" frame of each set always remains on top of its eight-frame sequence.

5. Place a clip binder on the left end of this frame stack. The clip should secure all of the frames in place.

6. Flip through the frames at a steady and quick rate. Notice how the frames blend into each other and produce what appears to be a smooth walking motion.

Deep Thoughts

Your brain can make up all sorts of things, such as excuses for missing homework assignments. But did you know that your brain creates a make-believe world that has the illusion of depth? That's right. What you think of as depth is a complete illusion!

ACTIVITY Fake Out

You can trick your brain into creating 3-D images by sending different 2-D views to each eye.

You Will Need

■ two sheets of paper
■ tape

1. Roll two sheets of paper into tubes. The tubes should be as wide as a large coin. Use tape to secure the tube shapes.

2. Hold the tubes as if they were a pair of binoculars. Place your hands over the end of each tube that you will bring over your eyes. These will form soft eye cups.

3. Position the other end of the tubes just above the image pairs on the opposite page. Raise the tubes so they are about 1 inch (2.5 cm) above the paper's surface. This will allow light to illuminate the pictures.

4. Look at the image pairs. Adjust the tubes' position so that only one image appears in each tube. Once you have parallel views of the side-by-side images, keep looking. As if by magic, the two separate images will appear to come together. When they fuse into a single image, the picture will take on a 3-D appearance.

Flat Screen Viewing

As you know, the curved end at the back of the eyeball is a flat surface. Therefore, any image that gets cast upon this screen is also flat. However, you "see" the world in

three dimensions. Your brain performs a bit of processing magic to change this 2-D image into an accurate 3-D representation of the real world.

In order to construct a mind's-eye view of depth, your brain uses various cues. Things such as speed, overlap, and brightness help create the trickery. However, the most important cue comes from seeing things with two eyes.

Hold up a finger. Shut one eye, then the other. Your finger appears to jump from each eye's slightly different view. It is this viewing difference that explains much of your brain's ability to "paint" things as 3-D onto flat scenes.

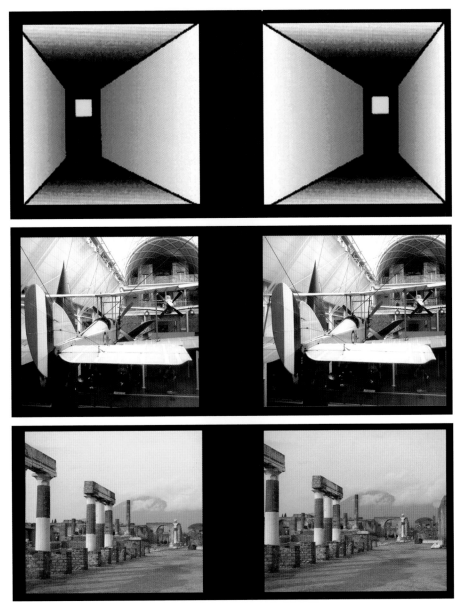

Sounding Off

Sound is all in your head. It doesn't exist outside of the sound-processing parts of your brain. Well, if it doesn't exist, what's out there? The answer is vibrations*. Strong vibrations. Weak vibrations. Rapid vibrations. Slow vibrations.

Vibrations that travel through the air move in sound waves. When a sound wave strikes your ear, a nerve signal is created. This signal travels along the auditory* nerve that goes from your ear to your brain.

Once it arrives in your brain, the signal is decoded into the sensation we know as sound. We place qualities such as loudness and pitch on these vibrations.

ACTIVITY Sounds Like

Things sound differently. This difference is used by your brain to tell things apart. Here's a fun activity that tests how well you can identify items by the sounds they make.

You Will Need

- several plastic film canisters (or something similar that can be opened and sealed shut)
- several grains of uncooked rice
- uncooked dried beans
- paper clips
- coins
- salt
- beads
- a friend

Fill each canister with a different item from the list. Challenge a friend to shake each container and, from the sound produced, identify the items within.

HOW TO SAY IT

vibrations:
vie-BRAY-shuns
auditory:
aw-deh-TOR-ee

ACTIVITY Two Ears Better Than One

Sound doesn't strike both of your ears at the same time. Instead, it reaches one ear a fraction of a second ahead of the other ear. This difference is used by your brain to help locate sounds. Without the two-ear advantage, it is much more difficult to judge the location of a sound.

You Will Need

- a pair of earmuffs
- chair
- ruler
- tape
- a friend
- a large room

1. Place the chair in the center of a large room.

2. Use your ruler to mark off a series of distances from the chair. The marks should be separated from each other by a distance of about 3 feet (1 meter).

3. Have your friend sit on the chair and face away from you. Standing at different marked distances from her, call out her name. She must "guesstimate" your distance.

4. Now have your friend put on a pair of earmuffs so that only one ear is covered. Once more, see if she can "guesstimate" your distance when you call her name. Can she better locate you using two ears or just one?

SUE !

Speaking of Survival

Although it doesn't sound like much, baby babble is part of our success as Earth's most intelligent species. Language is not something that's just *nice* to learn. It's something that is essential to learn. Just like strong muscles, sharp eyesight, and a grasping grip, communication is a survival adaptation of our species.

All babies are born with brains that are ready to learn to speak, listen, and understand. In fact, the coos of baby talk are babies' first attempts to reproduce patterns of speech. Even though they don't know what the words mean, they imitate speech to understand the structure of the sounds. That's why it is important to expose babies to language at a very young age.

There are isolated cases of children who have grown up in the wild and never communicated with other humans. Although their brains and hearing remained intact, these children were never able to learn human languages. Scientists think their ability to communicate was lost because, as infants, they were never exposed to speech. Most scientists think that by the time someone becomes a young adult, the ability to learn a first language is lost because

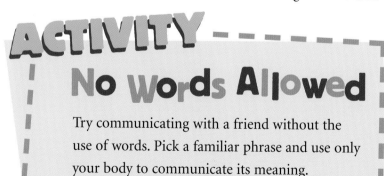

ACTIVITY
No Words Allowed

Try communicating with a friend without the use of words. Pick a familiar phrase and use only your body to communicate its meaning.

we "grow out of" the stage when we can easily learn new languages. The brain "rewires" and uses the speaking region for something else.

This Area Reserved

As you know, different areas of the brain process different thoughts. A region in the left hemisphere processes language. It doesn't matter if you hear words or see concepts communicated through sign language. These thoughts go to the same center in the brain. All humans are born with a region that is reserved for processing patterns of language. In deaf individuals, this area is used to process the meaning of sign language. In hearing individuals, the area is used to understand spoken words.

WIDER ON THE RIGHT?

Did you know that the right side of a person's mouth opens slightly more than the left side? That's because the language center is found in the left hemisphere of the brain. Since the left half of the brain controls the right half of the body, it has more influence in getting right-side muscles to move. Although this difference is difficult to notice in the normal speech of adults, it's easier to observe in babbling babies.

THE LOW NOTE ON THE MOZART EFFECT

The Mozart Effect is associated with a supposed increase in brain power that happens from listening to the music of Wolfgang Mozart. The scientists who uncovered this connection found that certain frequencies and patterns in music (and it doesn't *have* to be by Mozart) stimulate sites in the brain. As a result, some parents have music playing in their newborn's room. In addition to music helping their infant sleep, they believe that listening to it helps build nerve pathways in the child's brain. Whether listening to Mozart really makes you smarter is undecided, even by the scientists who first uncovered the connection. In spite of the controversy, many people seem to believe in the magic of Mozart.

Touchy Subject

Which of the following sensations are included in the sense of touch?

a. Temperature

b. Pressure

c. Movement

d. Pain

Answer: All of them! The sense that we call touch includes a variety of sensations. Each sensation is detected by its own special sensor. These sensors are just beneath the surface of the skin and are distributed all over your body.

Some parts of your body have a greater concentration of touch sensors. For example, your lips and hands have the greatest number of touch sensors. Your back has relatively few sensors.

ACTIVITY   The Alien Within

Check out this strange looking creature. It's called a homunculus*. A homunculus has a basic human form. The distorted size of the body parts reflect the concentration of touch sensors. The more sensors, the larger the body part. The fewer sensors, the smaller the part.

You Will Need

■ modeling clay

Create your own homunculus with modeling clay. Use this drawing as a guide to produce an accurate model of skin sensor concentration. As you can see from your model, lips and hands are very sensitive areas. They detect many different sensations that are important to our survival.

ACTIVITY Concentration

How sensitive to touch are different areas of your skin? You can uncover this in the following activity.

You Will Need

- large paper clip
- ruler

1. Unbend and straighten out a large paper clip. Then fold the clip so that the blunt ends are aligned and separated by about 1 inch (2.5 cm).

2. Gently touch the two ends of the clip to the fingertip of your index finger. Make sure that they make contact at the same time. While the tips are touching your skin, can you feel two distinct "touch spots"?

3. Rebend the clip so that the ends are now about 0.5 inches (about 1.3 cm) apart. Touch the same area of you skin. Can you still detect two separate touch spots, or have they blended into a single spot?

4. Keep testing your sensitivity as you decrease the distance between the tips. Record the closest distance that you can identify as two separate contact points.

5. Repeat the test using the exposed skin of your shoulder. Is your shoulder as sensitive as your fingertip?

homunculus:
hoh-MEN-cue-luss   HOW TO SAY IT

Communicating with Touch

In 1932, a communication system was standardized for the visually impaired. The system, named after the blind teenager who first introduced it, was called Braille.

Braille uses a pattern of raised dots to communicate the identity of letters and numbers. Each character is assigned a unique pattern of dots within a two-dot wide and three-dot high "cell." For example, the letter "a" is represented by a single raised dot in the top left position of the cell. The letter "l" is represented by three dots in the left column.

PLASTIC BRAIN

As you've learned, the brain is not fixed in the way it is organized. Experience can change the way it works. The brains of blind individuals may "reassign" the region that is ordinarily used for seeing. In these people, the "sight area" takes on the function of touch. Scientists have observed this switch of function using high-tech tools that identify regions of brain activity.

ACTIVITY Communicating with Braille

Here is the dot pattern that represents the Braille alphabet. Use it to create a basic message to a friend.

You Will Need

■ paper clip
■ index card or sheet of medium stock paper

Unbend the paper clip and use the end to carefully punch holes into an index card or a sheet of medium stock paper. Follow where the dots are positioned for each letter. Make sure your friend has a copy of the Braille alphabet so that she can decipher your message.

a b c d e f g

h i j k l m n

o p q r s t u

v w x y z . "

Tasty Smells

The sense of smell and the sense of taste are very closely related. Both sensations depend upon detecting chemicals in your environment. Smells are the sensations we get from chemicals that travel in the air. Tastes are sensations that are produced from chemicals in foods.

ACTIVITY Taste Confusion

Have you ever noticed that food lacks flavor when you are sick? If so, you're not alone. Most people find foods less flavorful when they are ill. That's because the aromas of the food may not move as freely through a stuffed or runny nose. Since you can't detect the smells, the intensity of the flavor is lessened.

You Will Need

■ different flavors of jelly beans

1. Hold your nose so that you can't smell the jelly beans.

2. Pick a color and place a jelly bean in your mouth. Begin chewing. What does it taste like?

3. Release your nose and breath normally. Take another jelly bean of the same flavor. Begin chewing. Can you taste the jellybean now?

Taste buds are groups of taste detectors that are arranged around the little bumps that you can see on your tongue. A person can have as many as 10,000 taste buds.

Each bud is specialized in what it can detect. Some taste buds produce signals that communicate a "bitter" sensation. Others produce "sweet" signals. Still others produce signals we associate with salty and sour tastes. Although the buds are mixed together, it seems that some regions of the tongue are more sensitive to certain tastes than others.

Death of a Taste Bud

Taste buds don't last forever. In fact, they are continually lost and replaced by new taste buds. How long do most taste buds last?

a. Less than 2 weeks.

b. About a month.

c. One year.

Answer: a. Most taste buds last for about 10 days. When they are gone, they are quickly replaced by new taste buds. However, as we age, this replacement process slows down. That's why older people seem to lose the ability to taste slight differences in foods.

HERE LIES **BUD** HE WAS SWEET, BUT SOMETIMES SOUR

Out of Body Experience

With your eyes closed, touch your fingertip to your nose. You probably succeeded because your brain knew where your finger and nose were. Without seeing these body parts, it was able to "best guess" their positions and guide them to meet.

The awareness of your body is part of the sense of self. This sense is a type of a mental map that keeps track of where body parts are and what they are doing. People who lose a limb, like an arm or a leg, often feel as if that body part is still there. This "phantom" limb sensation may be created by an intact "map" in the brain that continues to include the lost limb. The brain thinks the limb is still attached to the body and associates sensations (especially pain) with it.

ACTIVITY A Helping Hand

Like other senses, your sense of self can be tricked. The effect is so dramatic that you can be fooled into thinking a photo of a hand is actually a part of your body.

You Will Need

■ a friend

1. Place your right hand under the picture of the hand shown on the facing page. Make sure your palm is facing up.

2. Have a friend position one of her hands on your hidden right palm. Her other hand should be positioned on the picture.

3. Instruct your friend to stroke your hand with small and repeated movements. Make sure that you don't see her hand making these movements.

4. At the same time, your friend uses her hand to make the same movements on the page over the picture.

5. Concentrate on the picture of the hand and the repeated movements. Make sure that you don't see the same movements that are occurring beneath the page. You will only be feeling these movements.

6. After about 30 seconds, your brain will begin to get confused. Slowly, it will transfer your sensation of touch to the picture of the hand. As illogical as it sounds, your brain will think that the feelings are coming from the picture!

72

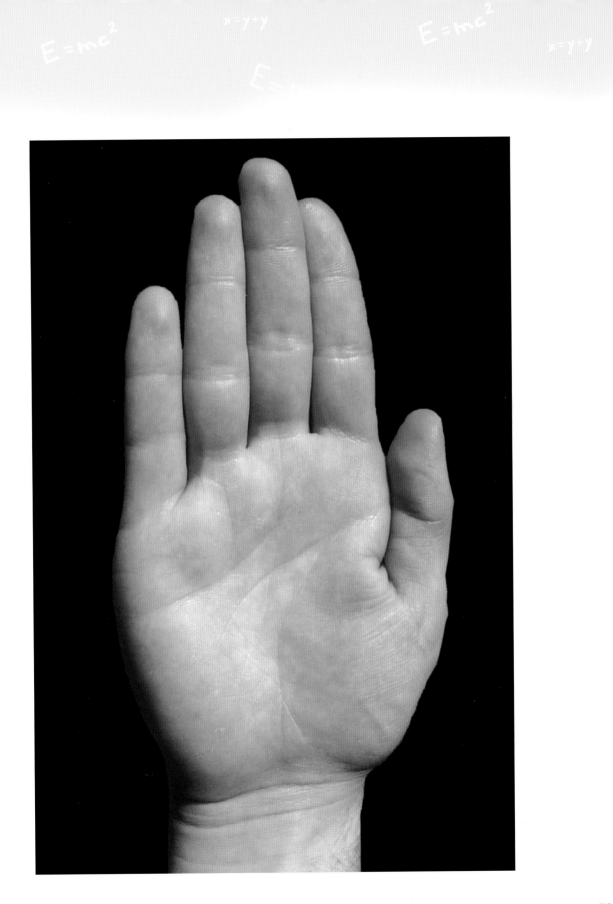

Girl Brains/Boy Brains

Have you ever wondered if boys and girls think differently? Well you are not alone. Scientists are also interested in whether being a male or being a female affects the way a person thinks.

Although research suggests that boys and girls may think differently, the differences are small. In fact, there is a greater difference in the way boys think among other boys, and the way girls think among other girls, than there is between boys and girls.

ACTIVITY Uncovering Hidden Objects

Here's a test that may show a difference in the way girls and boys think. Can you uncover a pentagon hidden in this jumble of lines?

Although the difference in finding the pentagon depends mostly upon individual skills, males seem to uncover the hidden shape sooner than females.

Answer on page 78.

ACTIVITY Find Out Yourself

Here's another test that may show a difference between boys and girls.

You Will Need

■ a sheet of paper
■ a watch or clock with a second hand

uncovering the switched pairs depends mostly upon individual skills, females seem to have a better memory for the placement of items than males.

1. Cover the block of pictures on the right with a sheet of paper before you have a chance to examine it.

2. Study the arrangement of pictures in the left block for 15 seconds.

3. Move the cover sheet from the right block to the left. Can you identify what pairs of objects exchanged positions?

Answer on page 78.

Once you know how this test works, develop a method for seeing if boys and girls perform differently on it. Test your family, friends, and classmates. Although the difference in

A Smarter Future

Science fiction movies sometimes show "big-brained" people from the future. In contrast to our normal head, these time-travelers have huge skulls packed with bigger and more powerful brains. Is that where people are headed? The answer is a definite "No way."

We are not evolving bigger heads or larger brains. The size of these body parts is set by our genes. In order to evolve bigger heads, there first has to be a random mutation for big heads. Presto! Offsprings are born with larger heads. Then, big head size has to produce a competitive edge by winning out over people with smaller heads. Without the mutation and competition, it appears that the head size of humans will remain pretty much the same.

You can, however, increase the power of your thinking without the need of any sci-fi gadgets or a larger brain. As we said in this book, whenever you think, you create signals that travel through your brain. Not only do these signals carry thoughts and messages, but they trigger the release of brain chemicals. These special chemicals cause brain cells to "sprout" new connections! And remember, it is these connections that produce the power of thinking.

Brain connections need a constant bath of these chemicals to remain healthy. If you don't use thinking pathways, you may not produce enough chemicals to maintain these links. In other words, you can lose some of the thinking power you have already constructed!

So keep making new connections and don't lose the links you've already created. Stay active and keep learning new things. The more you learn, the more your brain becomes (and remains) the site for powerful thinking.

Answers

Find the Right Person

e. President George W. Bush. However, his father, President George H.W. Bush was a lefty. Consider this: there are more lefty presidents than what might be expected by chance.

Puzzling Connections

Thirty-two paths.

IQ Test

1. KITTEN. The connection is adult to baby.

2. SHARK. It is the only animal with a backbone.

3. D. It is the only shape that contains curves.

4. 13. Each number equals the sum of the two previous numbers.

5. A. It is the only letter with a closed area.

6. CONTINENT. The letters rearrange into the word "Africa."

7. TWO. It takes each bird two hours to eat one worm.

8. SWITZERLAND. It has no shoreline on an ocean.

9. PRESERVES. The terms are related by the concentration of fruit.

10. E. It is the only figure that doesn't contain at least one colored-end block.

An Intelligent Assortment

Answers: 1c, 2d, 3a, 4g, 5h, 6e, 7b, 8f.

Riddle Me This

One. Only the poem's narrator was going to St. Ives.

Connect the Squares

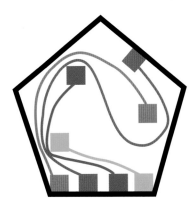

Riding a Horse

Line up the horses so that their backs are facing each other. Position the rider in between them.

Loop Trick

The answer lies in three carefully placed cuts. Make the cuts as shown, then twist one end of the strip halfway. Secure the loose ends to form this reality-twisting puzzle.

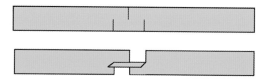

No Lifting Allowed

Think out of the box and beyond the pattern. You can connect all nine dots by extending lines outside the boundary you built into the puzzle.

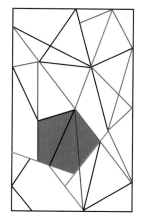

Uncovering Hidden Objects

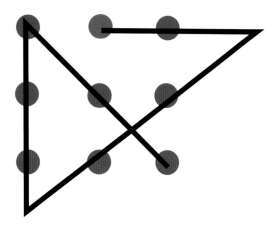

You are an Individual

No one else is like you on this entire planet. Therefore, don't let anyone set your limits or tell you what you can or cannot become.

Find Out Yourself

The school bus and fire engine are one pair. The hand and ear are the other pair.

About the Author

Michael Anthony DiSpezio is a renaissance educator who speaks, writes, and conducts teacher workshops throughout the world. He is the author of *Critical Thinking Puzzles, Great Critical Thinking Puzzles, Challenging Critical Thinking Puzzles, Visual Thinking Puzzles, Awesome Experiments in Electricity and Magnetism, Awesome Experiments in Force and Motion, Awesome Experiments in Light and Sound, Optical Illusion Magic, Simple Optical Illusion Experiments with Everyday Materials, Eye-Popping Optical Illusions, Map Mania, Dino Mania, Weather Mania, Space Mania*, and *Super Sensational Science Fair Projects* (all from  Sterling). He is also the co-author of over two dozen elementary, middle, and high school science textbooks and has been a "hired creative-gun" for clients including the Discovery Channel, MTV, and Children's Television Workshop. He also develops activities for the classroom guides to *Discover* magazine and *Scientific American Frontiers.*

These days, Michael is the curriculum architect for the JASON Academy, an on-line university that offers professional development courses for science teachers. When he's not writing, Michael is keynoting on subjects that include optical illusions, releasing inner creativity, and gender differences in the brain. You can find out more about his keynotes and audience presentations at www.premierespeakers.com.

Index